LEAVING MY

After the Journey

HOMELAND

Hoping for a Home After El Salvador

CRABTREE
PUBLISHING COMPANY
WWW.CRABTREEBOOKS.COM

Linda Barghoorn

CRABTREE
PUBLISHING COMPANY
WWW.CRABTREEBOOKS.COM

Author: Linda Barghoorn

Editors: Sarah Eason, Harriet McGregor, and Janine Deschenes

Proofreader and indexer: Wendy Scavuzzo

Editorial director: Kathy Middleton

Design: Paul Myerscough and Jessica Moon

Photo research: Rachel Blount

Production coordinator and Prepress technician: Ken Wright

Print coordinator: Katherine Berti

Consultant: Hawa Sabriye

Written, developed, and produced by Calcium

Publisher's Note: The story presented in this book is a fictional account based on extensive research of real-life accounts by refugees, with the aim of reflecting the true experience of refugee children and their families.

Photo Credits:
t=Top, c=Center, b=Bottom, l= Left, r=Right

Cover: Shutterstock: carlos.araujo

Inside: Shutterstock: Aberu.Go: p. 19t; Anton Ivanov: p. 5r; Atlaspix: p. 5cl; Brgfx: p. 6t; Rob Byron: p. 10b; Jose Carrera: p. 25c; ChameleonsEye: p. 24c; Cobisimo: p. 24t; Elena Diego Photography: p. 17c; Diego Drenoso: p. 20; Elenabsl: p. 20t; Fishman64: p. 26b; GlobalVision 360: p. 6t; HappyPictures: p. 12b; Vic Hinterlang: p. 7t, 10t, 11l, 13b, 14b, 26c; Simone Hogan: p. 23c; Illpaxphotomatic: pp. 12-13; IsoVector: p. 18b, 22-23b; Ruslana Iurchenko: pp. 16-17t; Helga Khorimarko: pp. 18l, 19r, 21r; Lawkeeper: p. 23tr; Cindy Lee: p. 26bl; LineTale: p. 11r; Ian MacLellan: pp. 6b, 9tl, 22t; Macrovector: p. 7c, 23cr; Estudio Maia: p. 1l; Mspoint: p. 28t; MSSA: p. 11bl; Nong Vector Design: p. 16c; NotionPic: p. 22bl; Parose: pp. 3, 14t; Photoroyalty: p. 10bl; Photoshooter2015: p. 18; Joseph Sorrentino: pp. 14c, 21c; Ulrike Stein: p. 15; Stockakia: p. 16b; Sudowoodo: p. 29t; Globe Turner: p. 5tl; What's My Name: pp. 25b, 27t, 27r; Yoko Design: p. 1bg© UNHCR: © UNHCR/Marta Martinez: p. 27c; © UNHCR/Daniele Volpe: pp. 28b, 29c; Wikimedia Commons: U.S. Customs and Border Protection: p. 9r.

Library and Archives Canada Cataloguing in Publication

Title: Hoping for a home after El Salvador / Linda Barghoorn.
Names: Barghoorn, Linda, author.
Series: Leaving my homeland: after the journey.
Description: Series statement: Leaving my homeland : after the journey | Includes index.
Identifiers: Canadiana (print) 20190114819 | Canadiana (ebook) 20190114835 | ISBN 9780778765004 (softcover) | ISBN 9780778764946 (hardcover) | ISBN 9781427123749 (HTML)
Subjects: LCSH: Refugees—El Salvador—Juvenile literature. | LCSH: Refugees—United States—Juvenile literature. | LCSH: Refugee children—El Salvador—Juvenile literature. | Refugee children—United States—Juvenile literature. | LCSH: Refugees—Social conditions—Juvenile literature. | LCSH: El Salvador—History—1992—Juvenile literature. | LCSH: El Salvador—Social conditions—Juvenile literature.
Classification: LCC HV640.5.S24 B37 2019 | DDC j305.23086/914097284—dc23

Library of Congress Cataloging-in-Publication Data

Names: Barghoorn, Linda, author.
Title: Hoping for a home after El Salvador / Linda Barghoorn.
Description: New York : Crabtree Publishing Company, [2019] | Series: Leaving my homeland: after the journey | Includes index.
Identifiers: LCCN 2019023036 (print) | LCCN 2019023037 (ebook) | ISBN 9780778764946 (hardback) | ISBN 9780778765004 (paperback) | ISBN 9781427123749 (ebook)
Subjects: LCSH: Refugees--El Salvador--Juvenile literature. | Refugees--Mexico--Juvenile literature. | Refugee children--El Salvador--Juvenile literature. | Refugee children--Mexico--Juvenile literature. | Immigrants--Government policy--United States--Juvenile literature. | United States--Emigration and immigration--Government policy--Juvenile literature.
Classification: LCC HV640.5.S24 B37 2019 (print) | LCC HV640.5.S24 (ebook) | DDC 362.7/7914089687284072--dc23
LC record available at https://lccn.loc.gov/2019023036
LC ebook record available at https://lccn.loc.gov/2019023037

Crabtree Publishing Company
www.crabtreebooks.com   1-800-387-7650

Printed in the U.S.A./082019/CG20190712

Published in Canada
Crabtree Publishing
616 Welland Ave.
St. Catharines, Ontario
L2M 5V6

Published in the United States
Crabtree Publishing
PMB 59051
350 Fifth Avenue, 59th Floor
New York, New York 10118

Published in the United Kingdom
Crabtree Publishing
Maritime House
Basin Road North, Hove
BN41 1WR

Published in Australia
Crabtree Publishing
Unit 3 – 5 Currumbin Court
Capalaba
QLD 4157

What Is in This Book?

Benito's Story: From El Salvador to Mexico

Hello! My name is Benito. I was born in El Salvador. I grew up in a large family. My aunties, uncles, cousins, and grandparents all lived nearby. We saw one another all the time. We were such a close family.

When I was 11 years old, life became dangerous and difficult. **Gang** members began to threaten us. One gang demanded that my father pay them money. But no matter how much money we paid, the gang always wanted more. When my father could not pay, the men said they would hurt us. One day, my brother, Juan, disappeared. The gang said my sister, Gabriela, and I would be next. We were so afraid that we left our country. We became **refugees** and fled to Mexico. But it hurt us to leave without knowing what happened to Juan.

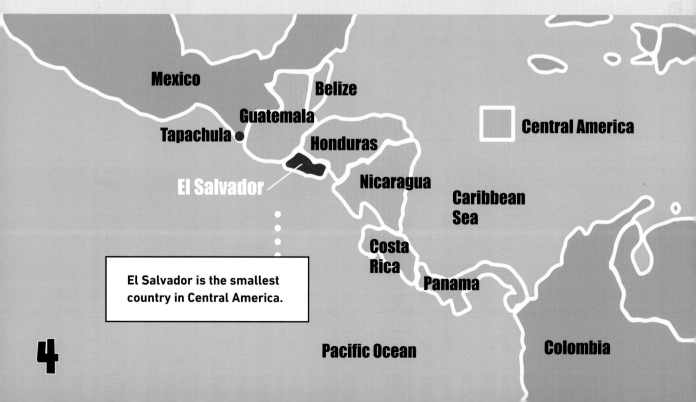

Mexico

Belize

Guatemala

Tapachula •

Honduras

Central America

El Salvador

Nicaragua

Caribbean Sea

Costa Rica

Panama

Pacific Ocean

Colombia

El Salvador is the smallest country in Central America.

You have the **right** to a home, an education, and freedom to practice your religion and identity. If you are denied these rights in your **homeland**, you have the right to seek safety in another country. While you read through this book, think about these rights.

Mexico's flag

El Salvador's flag

Towns like this in southern Mexico have seen the arrival of many refugees from Central America.

*Now we live outside the city of Tapachula in Mexico. It is near the **border** with Guatemala. My parents have found jobs. But often there is not enough money for food, clothes, and school supplies. I go to school with my sisters and brother. The local children bully us. They tell us to go back home to El Salvador and take our problems with us.*

The gangs that we fled from in El Salvador are also here in Mexico. But it is still too dangerous to return to El Salvador. We now dream of a brighter future somewhere else.

My Homeland, El Salvador

For hundreds of years, most people in El Salvador were farmers and lived simple lives. Although it was a poor country, people lived there peacefully. But modern El Salvador is troubled. Half of its people live in the countryside, in homes with no running water or electricity. Those who have moved to the cities have often found it difficult to get jobs. Many people there live in a world of violence and **poverty**.

The people in El Salvador live in fear of powerful gangs, known as maras. Maras make money from the **illegal trade** of guns and drugs. They fight one another for control of this trade. They demand money and cooperation from **citizens**, and threaten people who do not agree. They often **recruit** or force children to join the gangs. Other people choose to join gangs because they offer belonging and money. People who join may be from very poor families, or have no family at all.

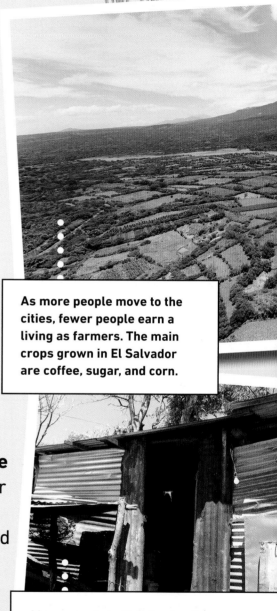

As more people move to the cities, fewer people earn a living as farmers. The main crops grown in El Salvador are coffee, sugar, and corn.

Many people in El Salvador live in poverty. Many businesses are threatened by gangs. In recent years, crops have been damaged by disease and changes in temperature and weather. This means that a lot of people in El Salvador do not make enough money to meet their basic needs.

These refugees are from El Salvador. They are resting at a temporary shelter in Mexico, which has been set up in a sports field.

All of the gang activity means that life in El Salvador is surrounded by violence. Everyone in the country knows someone who has been hurt by the gangs. Parents worry that they cannot protect their children from the gangs. Some pay **smugglers** to get their children out of El Salvador.

Story in Numbers

Around

6.5 million

people live in El Salvador. An estimated

500,000

citizens are involved in gangs. These gangs are responsible for about 1.5 murders involving children each day across the country.

Benito's Story: Leaving My Homeland

My sisters, my brother, and I were so afraid when we left our home. We asked our parents many questions. Where were we going? What would it be like? How would Juan ever find us if we are so far from home? We were not given many answers.

Since arriving in Mexico two years ago, we have watched the news whenever we can. We have seen things in El Salvador get worse. The government does not seem able to stop the gangs. Many more families have left the country, too.

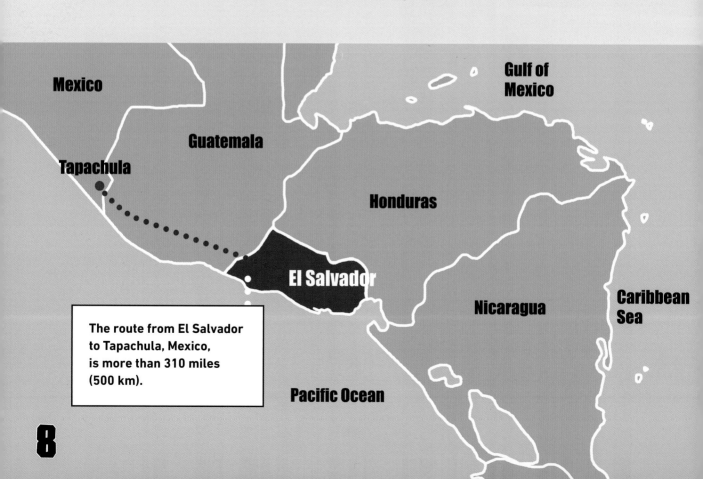

Mexico

Gulf of Mexico

Guatemala

Tapachula

Honduras

El Salvador

Caribbean Sea

Nicaragua

The route from El Salvador to Tapachula, Mexico, is more than 310 miles (500 km).

Pacific Ocean

In many places along the border between the United States and Mexico, walls are being built to keep migrants from crossing into the United States.

Children in El Salvador want the same things as children everywhere else: to grow up peacefully, surrounded by friends and family.

My parents often talk to my aunt, Lara. She runs our family's store back home. The gang that threatened us beat her when she could not pay them. Her eldest son, my cousin Luis, joined one of the gangs to protect his family. But he was killed by a **rival** gang. Aunt Lara has told my parents she is making plans to leave. She cannot bear the thought of her other son, Cesar, being attacked by a gang. Cesar and I are close cousins. He wrote to me to tell me of their plans.

Aunt Lara says people in San Salvador are talking about joining a **caravan** to get to the United States. The caravan will have to travel a long way through Mexico. My parents worry about Aunt Lara and Cesar's safety during the long journey.

A New Life

Mexico does not have a lot of money. It is difficult for the country to provide thousands of refugees with basic services, such as education and health care. The refugees seek shelter in Mexico or pass through on their way to the United States. Mexico often struggles to help refugees, while dealing with its own issues of crime, poverty, and housing shortages.

Asylum seekers, or refugees who wish to stay in Mexico, face many challenges. Often, they find Mexico just as dangerous as the country they fled. Many of the gangs from Central America also move across the border with Mexico. These gangs threaten families who have fled. They also target family members who stayed behind in their homeland.

These Salvadoran refugees wait for trucks to take them to the next stop on their route to the United States.

Mexican gangs often target vulnerable migrants in poor neighborhoods. They recruit children as drug traffickers and force families to pay money to protect other family members in their home country from violence.

UN Rights of the Child

You have the right to special protection and help if you are a refugee.

Refugees may be afraid to reach out for help. They fear **discrimination** by local citizens. They must compete with local people for housing, jobs, and places in schools. Jobs can be difficult to find and often pay so poorly that it is hard to support a family. In Mexico, a job on a farm or in **construction** might pay only 150 pesos ($8) a day.

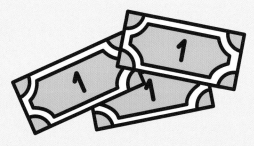

Government programs support asylum seekers, but they are limited and are not easy to find. International and local organizations, such as the **United Nations High Commissioner for Refugees (UNHCR)** or neighborhood schools and churches, help support asylum seekers. They help find jobs for adults and places for families to live. They also help refugees fill out important paperwork when they ask for asylum.

This refugee child fled poverty in El Salvador. He has been given a meal by the local church in Oaxaca, Mexico.

11

Benito's Story: Arriving in Mexico

When we were granted asylum in Mexico, my family was so relieved. We thought we were finally safe. But Mother still worried about Juan. How could we get news of him when we were so far away? Would he be able to join us if we learned he was still alive?

Other families from El Salvador live close by. We do not spend much time with them. Mother and Father have learned that gang members from our homeland are present in our neighborhood. It is difficult to tell who they are. Mother warns me to be careful about how I choose my friends.

This legal border crossing between El Salvador and Mexico buzzes with activity. Thousands of people pass through every day on their way to work, to shop, or to visit family and friends.

Hola Cesar!
How are you? Are you still planning to leave El Salvador? I still have nightmares about the night we crossed the river into Mexico. The water was so black. I thought it would swallow us up. When we got to land, we were arrested by the police. At first, they treated us like criminals. But after hearing our story, they let us stay here. I miss you so much and hope we can be together again! Benito

Maria is a volunteer from a nearby church. She visits us each week. Sometimes she brings food or clothes. She told Father about a place where they teach refugees to repair bicycles. Now Father spends two days a week working there. But the pay is not enough. When he is not there, he is always looking for other work.

These asylum seekers are lining up to apply to stay in Mexico. They face long lines and uncertain futures.

Story in Numbers

In 2018, the number of asylum claims in Mexico rose to more than

29,000.

This is double the previous year. Applications by refugees from El Salvador rose by 112% in the first three months of 2019.

A New Home

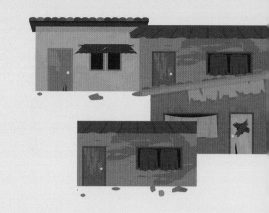

Mexico does not have enough housing even for its own citizens. In some cities, tiny houses, called *mini casas* have been built to create more places to live. Families squeeze into these living spaces. They are unsafe because they are overcrowded and poorly built.

When they first arrive in Mexico, refugees live in **migrant centers**. Sometimes the centers are so crowded that they cannot take all of the refugees. People are released with no help or support. They must find enough money on their own to live nearby while they wait to hear whether they are allowed to stay. The government is supposed to make decisions within 90 days. But it often takes much longer.

These refugees share lunch at a shelter while they wait for the Mexican government to decide if they can stay in the country.

This man, who has fled his homeland, is using scrap materials to build his own temporary shelter in Oaxaca.

UN Rights of the Child

You have the right to live in a clean and safe environment. The government has an obligation to help you if you are poor or in need of support.

Gangs operate freely in city slums like this one, where they are hard to identify and difficult for police to arrest.

Refugees must quickly find jobs to support their families. Many do not have the necessary skills to get jobs. So, they must attend training classes to learn new skills. Others accept low-paying jobs. But this makes it difficult to afford proper housing. They are forced into crowded, poor areas called slums. Large numbers of refugees live in inexpensive housing there—but they are vulnerable to crime and poverty.

Benito's Story: My New Home

Our neighborhood is so different from the one we left behind. In El Salvador, our home was on a quiet village street. There were green fields all around us. Here, we live in a crowded, dirty, noisy neighborhood. It is on the edge of the city.

Our home is made of mud bricks. Some of the bricks have cracked, so the walls leak when it rains. Many of the houses around us are painted yellow, blue, or white. But the colors are faded and peeling. Our house needs the walls repaired and a new coat of paint. But Mother says we cannot afford it.

Sometimes, several families are forced to share a crowded home as they start life over in a new country.

Story in Numbers

The United States has refused many asylum seekers from Central America. This means more people are claiming asylum in Mexico. The figure rose from 2,000 in 2014 to more than **14,000 in 2017.**

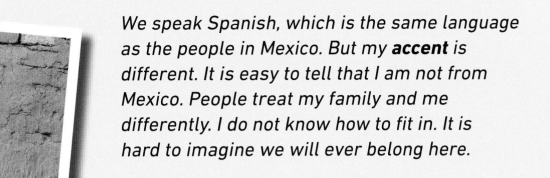

We speak Spanish, which is the same language as the people in Mexico. But my **accent** is different. It is easy to tell that I am not from Mexico. People treat my family and me differently. I do not know how to fit in. It is hard to imagine we will ever belong here.

Adobe bricks are used to make some homes in Mexico. Adobe is a mixture of clay, sand, straw, and water.

1

Hola Cesar!

Our home is so small and crowded. Mother sleeps with my sisters in one room. I share a room with Father and Mateo. The gangs we escaped in El Salvador are here, too. Last week, a boy threatened me with a knife. I escaped, but now I am nervous when I walk to school. Father wonders if we should move somewhere safer. But where should we go? It seems that nowhere is safe. Benito

A New School

Attending school in El Salvador can be dangerous. Gang members often control students' neighborhoods, hang out on school grounds, and walk the school hallways. Every day in El Salvador, a student is threatened or recruited by a gang member. To keep their children safe, many families have taken them out of school. Often, these children then fall behind in their schoolwork.

Walking to school in El Salvador often means crossing gang territory, where students may be threatened or even killed.

UN Rights of the Child

You have the right to a good education. You should be allowed to pursue the highest level of education possible to achieve your goals.

City schools, such as the one at the bottom of this photograph in Mexico City, often have more money than poorer schools in the countryside. They are able to offer students a better standard of education.

Refugee children in migrant centers in Mexico often fall even further behind. Before they are allowed to attend school in Mexico, they must be given asylum. But it often takes a very long time to get asylum. There are few tools available to help them catch up once they do continue their education.

Refugees hope for a better education in Mexico for their children. They are often disappointed. Mexico struggles with many of the same issues as El Salvador. Schools and classrooms, especially outside of cities, do not have many supplies. There are few trained teachers, and gangs often threaten students.

Drop-out rates are high in Mexico. Many people there cannot read. Most Mexican children finish primary school, but many do not graduate from high school.

Benito's Story: My New School

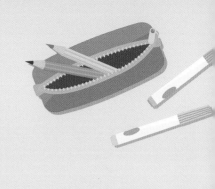

I have to wear a uniform at my new school. It is old and does not fit me well at all. But we have no money for a new one. There are not enough teachers at my school. So, my school has morning and afternoon shifts. I can only go to school in the afternoon, from 1:30 p.m. until 6:00 p.m. There is no bus, so Gabriela and I walk 30 minutes to school. In the winter, school closes earlier so we can get home safely before dark. We need to avoid the gangs.

Students that go to small rural, or country, schools may attend classes outdoors.

The laptops in our classroom are old. They only work sometimes. Some of our books have pages missing. One thing I love at school is playing soccer with my friends. A boy in my class brings a ball to school and we play soccer at recess.

Story in Numbers

While 9 out of 10 children attend primary school in Mexico, only about

1 in 4

will finish high school.

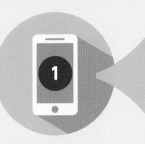

Hola Cesar!

I have been working hard to catch up on my schoolwork since we arrived here. But last month, our teacher did not even show up for two weeks. He had not been paid by the government. How will I ever learn enough to graduate from high school? Mother and Father say that you and Aunt Lara plan to join a migrant caravan so that you can travel to the United States. Maybe we will meet when your caravan travels through Mexico! Benito

Students enjoy a few moments of fun in a quick game of soccer after school.

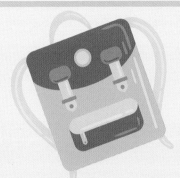

When I arrived home from school last week, Mother and Father were talking about Aunt Lara. They sounded very excited. She had told them that she soon will be joining a migrant caravan with Cesar. They will travel through Mexico to reach the United States. There, they will apply for asylum. We are talking about the idea of joining them. We could all build a new life in the United States.

On the Move

It takes a lot of courage to leave everything behind to start over in a new country. Many people in Central America feel their governments are unable to protect them. They feel their only option for safety is to leave. When they cannot afford to travel together, families send their children on the journey alone. But children are often targeted by gangs, especially when they travel alone.

In 2018, refugees from El Salvador, Honduras, and Guatemala formed a big migrant caravan. They hoped that, as a large group, they could travel more safely. They also hoped to pressure the United States' government into giving them asylum. That would give them a chance for safety and a better future.

More than 36 percent of people living in rural parts of El Salvador live in extreme poverty.

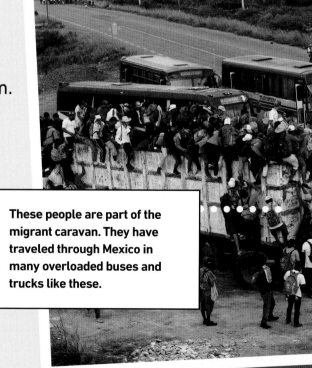

These people are part of the migrant caravan. They have traveled through Mexico in many overloaded buses and trucks like these.

The U.S. government claimed the asylum seekers were trying to cross its borders illegally. But asylum seekers have the legal right to protection as they escape violence in their homelands.

More and more refugees joined the caravan as it moved toward Mexico. Many were vulnerable women and children. They walked for weeks, stopping only to rest and eat.

The U.S. government did not want to accept the refugees. It said that **illegal immigrants** are bringing violence and crime into their country. It warned all caravans to turn back. It threatened to push them back by force if they tried to cross the border without permission. As the caravan reached the U.S. border, thousands of people were forced to wait in makeshift camps as they applied for asylum.

Benito's Story: My New Way of Life

We spend a lot of our days thinking about Aunt Lara and her journey. Aunt Lara spoke to Mother and Father before she left home to join the migrant caravan as it passed through El Salvador. She was filled with hope about getting to the United States. We watched on TV as the caravan grew larger and got nearer to Mexico.

Many areas in Mexico suffer from poverty and crime. Some Mexicans worry that their country will not be able to support the caravan's asylum seekers. Others believe the asylum seekers bring crime and violence from their homelands.

Story in Numbers

The migrant caravan traveled from Honduras to the border with the United States. This dangerous journey covered more than

2,670 miles
(4,300 km).

The president of the United States says refugees want to destroy his country. He warned the caravan to turn back. Father is frustrated. He does not know why the American government is so angry and worried about the caravan. He wonders how such a rich and powerful country can be afraid of poor refugees. Like us, all the refugees want is to escape poverty and dangerous gangs.

Hola Benito! We left El Salvador two weeks ago to join the caravan. Have you seen it on the news? Soon we will cross into Mexico. We are tired and hungry. Sometimes, we have been able to sleep in temporary shelters. Other times, we have had to sleep outside. Some people have been so kind to us, offering us food when we pass through their village. Hope to see you soon! Cesar

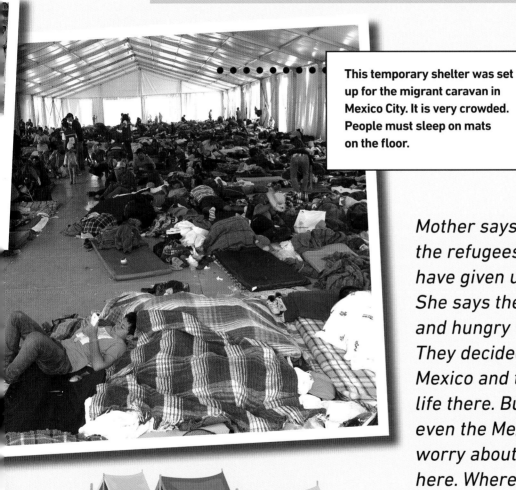

This temporary shelter was set up for the migrant caravan in Mexico City. It is very crowded. People must sleep on mats on the floor.

Mother says that some of the refugees in the caravan have given up their journey. She says they were too tired and hungry to continue. They decided to stay in Mexico and try to build a life there. But I know that even the Mexican people worry about having us here. Wherever we go now, I hear people whisper a lot of bad things about us.

Benito's Story: Looking to the Future

Mother and Father continued to watch the news on TV. The caravan was getting near the U.S. border. They texted Aunt Lara every day. They were so worried. Some days, Aunt Lara cried because the journey was so difficult, but she was determined not to give up.

At last, Aunt Lara and Cesar got to the U.S. border. It had taken them almost two months. Mother and Father explained that they had to wait in a migrant camp for an interview with U.S. immigration workers. But as they waited, more and more refugees arrived. The camp grew into a crowded, dirty, and dangerous tent city.

Some children have been separated from their parents at the U.S. border.

Migrants who cross illegally into the United States from Mexico are often sent to prisons, like this one, if they are caught.

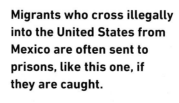

UN Rights of the Child

You have the right to an identity, which no one can take away from you.

*Aunt Lara says that everyone in the tent city is very impatient now. The U.S. government has delayed and refused asylum applications. When some tried to cross the U.S. border, guards fired **tear gas** to push them back. Aunt Lara does not know what to do. She is relying on volunteers for food, clothing, and shelter. She does not know how long they can stay in the tent city.*

This mural, painted by 24 female asylum seekers from Central America, represents grief for the families they have left behind, peace for their countries, and hope for the future.

Life here in Mexico is hard. Mother and Father have little hope for the future. We are proud Salvadorans. But we know we cannot go home yet. We are waiting to see if Aunt Lara reaches the United States. Then, Father says, maybe we can apply to join her there. But Mother worries we will never find Juan if we move to the United States. I do not know what will happen. I just hope that things become easier for people like us.

Do Not Forget Our Stories!

Poverty, violence, and discrimination have forced millions of children and families to flee their homes in countries around the world. They try to escape danger and often face frightening and uncertain futures.

In Mexico, organizations such as the Mexican Commission for Refugee Assistance (COMAR) help refugees find jobs and places to live. The immigration rights group Sin Fronteras works to improve **human rights** for refugees and migrants in Mexico. Its name means "Without Borders." Many local churches support refugees. They give them food and clothing donations. In neighborhoods where asylum seekers gather, they can provide one another with support and friendship.

These refugee brothers are receiving help from a UNHCR protection officer in Tapachula, Mexico. They fled from gangs in El Salvador.

UN Rights of the Child

You have the right to live in freedom and to pursue the best future possible.

This lady is a Salvadoran refugee in Mexico. She is taking care of her neighbor's child as a part-time job.

Refugee children want the same things as everyone else. They want a safe home, healthy food, an education, and the opportunity to reach their goals. They are often quick to adapt to their new culture, learn the language, and make new friends. They enjoy sharing the food, culture, and language of their homeland. As you read more about their stories, think about how you can help refugees in your own community and around the world.

Discussion Prompts

1. What difficulties do refugees face when they flee El Salvador and travel to Mexico?
2. Mexico is a host country and an **origin country** for refugees. How do you think this affects life in Mexico?
3. Why might host countries not want refugees to come there?

Glossary

accent A way of speaking a language

asylum Protection given to refugees by a country

border Line separating two countries

caravan Group of people traveling together

citizens Persons who belong to a country and have the right to that country's protection

construction Building work

culture The shared beliefs, values, customs, traditions, arts, and ways of life of a particular group of people

discrimination Unfair treatment of someone because of their race, religion, ethnic group, or other identifiers

gang Organized group of criminals

homeland The country where someone was born or grew up

human rights Rights that belong to every person

illegal Not allowed by law

illegal immigrants People who leave one country and enter another country against the law

migrant centers Places where migrants are held while their asylum applications are processed

origin country The country that a person is from or was born in

poverty The state of being very poor and having few belongings

recruit Persuade to work for someone

refugees People who flee from their own country to another due to unsafe conditions

right A privilege or freedom protected by law

rival Someone in competition for the same goal

smugglers People who move people or things illegally

tear gas A gas that causes severe irritation to the eyes

trade Purchase and sale of goods or services

traffickers People who illegally move people or drugs for money

United Nations High Commissioner for Refugees (UNHCR) A program that protects and supports refugees everywhere

vulnerable At risk of harm

Learning More

Books

Mattern, Joanne. *El Salvador* (All Around the World). Pogo Publisher, 2019.

Paul, Miranda, and Baptiste Paul. *Adventures to School: Real-Life Journeys of Students from Around the World.* Little bee books, 2018.

Penfold, Alexandra. *All Are Welcome.* Knopf Books for Young Readers, 2018.

Tafolla, Carmen. *What Can You Do with a Paleta?* Dragonfly Books, 2014.

Websites

www.amnesty.org.uk/files/2017-06/Activity%20-%20Seeking%20safety.pdf?QEgP75_LXPGt0d91YCDXgx0efPQ4Sl3u=
Scroll to pages 5 and 6 for facts and figures about refugees, then try some of the activities.

https://easyscienceforkids.com/all-about-el-salvador
Learn some interesting facts about El Salvador's geography.

www.unicef.org/rightsite/files/uncrcchilldfriendlylanguage.pdf
Learn more about the UN Convention on the Rights of the Child.

www.unhcr.org/teaching-about-refugees.html#words
Visit this page for an explanation of many words related to being a refugee.

Index

About the Author

Linda Barghoorn studied languages in university because she wanted to travel the world. She has visited 60 countries, taking photographs and writing stories about the people and cultures of our planet. At home, she volunteers at a local agency that provides newcomers and their families with clothing and community support.